ONE❀DAY
Easter Crafts

Publications International, Ltd.

Copyright © 1994 Publications International, Ltd. All rights reserved. This book may not be reproduced or quoted in whole or in part by mimeograph or any other printed or electronic means, or for presentation on radio, television, videotape, or film without written permission from:

Louis Weber, C.E.O.
Publications International, Ltd.
7373 N. Cicero Avenue
Lincolnwood, Illinois 60646

Permission is never granted for commercial purposes.

Manufactured in U.S.A.

8 7 6 5 4 3 2 1

ISBN 0-7853-0121-6

Craft Designers: Ginger Kean Berk, Bev George, Maria Nerius, Betty Valle, and Karen Ann Wiant

Contributing Writer: Betty Valle

Technical Advisor: Pamela A. Zimny

Photography: Sacco Productions Limited/Chicago

Photographer: Peter Ross

Production: Roberta Ellis

Photo Stylist: Hilary Rose/With Style

Location Scouting: Sally Mauer/With Style

Models: Karen Blaschek, Lisa Bruno/Royal Model Management, and Veronica Franz/Stewart Talent Management

Photo Site Acknowledgements: Sweet Basil Hill Farm Bed & Breakfast, represented by B&B MidWest Reservations

Cover and inside illustration (background pattern): Courtesy of the Victoria and Albert Museum, London

The mention of any product is merely a record of the procedure used and does not constitute an endorsement by the respective proprietors of Publications International, Ltd., nor does it constitute an endorsement by any of these companies that their products should be used in the manner recommended by this publication.

Sources of Materials:

Aldastar Corp. poms, 51, 59. **Aleene's Designer tacky glue,** 22, 27. **Barry Products Co.** chenille and glitter poms, 51. **Black & Decker** 2-temp glue gun, 11, 51, 56, 59. **Bond Adhesives Company** 527 Multi-Purpose Cement, 42. **Classic Elite Yarns, Inc.** BY HAND yarn, 24. **Concord** fabrics, 54. **Craf-t Products** chalks, 11, 51, 59. **Delta Technical Coatings, Inc.** Creamcoat paint, 32, 42. **Fairfield Processing Corporation** poly-fil, 11. **Fiskars, Inc.** scissors, 14, 16, 18, 20, 24, 30, 32, 42, 54, 56. **Forster Manufacturing Co.** craft sticks, 11. **J. & P. Coates** threads, 54, 56. **Jones Tones** fabric paint and glitter, 48. **Loew Cornell** brushes and styluses, 14, 32, 38, 42, 48. **Michaels Easter Collection** plastic eggs, 59. **Olfa** rotary cutter, 56. **Omnigrid Inc.** ruler, 56. **Pellon Division Freudenberg Non-Wovens Ltd.,** 56. **Provo Craft** wood bunny, 51. **Putnam Company, Inc.** fiberfill, 54. **Sahara** florists foam, 27. **Sew-Art International** stabilizer, 56. **Sharpie** permanent markers, 38. **Sulky** iron-on transfer pens, 38, 48. **Tulip Productions** fabric paints, 38, 59. **Walnut Hollow** wooden products, 14, 42. **Westrim** fun foam, 11, 51. **Wimpole Street Creations** stuffed bunnies, 16, 18. **Woodworks** wood eggs and bodies, 51, 59. **Wm. E. Wright Ltd.** trims and ribbons, 11, 16, 20, 54, 56. **Uchida of America, Corp.** fabric markers, 38, 48.

Table of Contents

Introduction

Springtime, flowers, bunnies, babies—all the
joys of Eastertide! Bring them all into your
house with One-Day Easter Crafts.
With many different projects and crafts to
choose from, you'll find many projects to make
for your home or to give as gifts. You'll find
stitching, sewing, and painting crafts.
We hope you enjoy creating these projects.
They are for all skill levels and interests.
You'll find that many of the projects use basic
items you already have around your home.
Once you begin, you'll see that creating your
own gifts and holiday decorations is a satisfing
and relaxing way to get ready for Easter!

What You'll Find

Cross-Stitch

Cross-stitch is traditionally worked on an "even-weave" cloth that has vertical and horizontal threads of equal thickness and spacing. Six-strand embroidery floss is used for most stitching; there are also many beautiful threads that can be used to enhance the appearance of the stitching. Finishing and framing a counted cross-stitch piece will complete your work. There are many options in framing—just visit your local craft shop or framing gallery.

Basic Supplies

Fabric: The most common even-weave fabric is 14-count Aida cloth. The weave of this fabric creates distinct squares that make stitching very easy for the beginner.

Needles, Hoops, and Scissors: A blunt-end or tapestry needle is used for counted cross-stitch. A #24 needle is the recommended size for stitching on 14-count Aida cloth. You may use an embroidery hoop while stitching—just be sure to remove it when not working on your project. A small pair of sharp scissors is a definite help when working with embroidery floss.

Floss: Six-strand cotton embroidery floss is most commonly used, and it's usually cut into 18-inch lengths for stitching. Use two of the six strands for stitching on 14-count Aida cloth. Also use two strands for backstitching.

Preparing to Stitch

The pattern in this book will tell you what size the overall stitched area will be when completed. It will also tell you what size piece of material to use.

To locate the center of the design, lightly fold your fabric in half and in half again. Find the center of the chart by following the arrows on the sides.

Reading the chart is easy, since each square on the chart equals one stitch on the fabric. The colors correspond to the floss numbers listed in the color key. Select a color and stitch all of that color within an area. Begin

by holding the thread ends behind the fabric until secured or covered over with two or three stitches. You may skip a few stitches on the back of the material, but do not run the thread from one area to another behind a section that will not be stitched in the finished piece—it will show through the fabric. If your thread begins to twist, drop the needle and allow the thread to untwist. It is important to the final appearance of the project to keep an even tension when pulling stitches through so that all stitches will have a uniform look. To end a thread, weave or run the thread under several stitches on the back side. Cut the ends close to the fabric.

Each counted cross-stitch is represented by a colored square on the project's chart. For horizontal rows, work the stitches in two steps, i.e., all of the left to right stitches and then all of the right to left stitches (see figure A). For vertical rows, work each complete stitch as shown in figure B. Three-quarter stitches are often used when the design requires two colors in one square or to allow more detail in the pattern (see figure C.) The backstitch is often used to outline or create letters, and is shown by bold lines on the patterns. Backstitch is usually worked after the pattern is completed (see figure D.)

Figure A
Cross-stitch

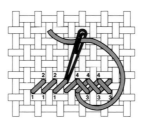

Figure B
Vertical cross-stitch

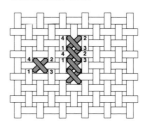

Figure C
Three-quarter stitches

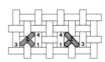

Figure D
Backstitching

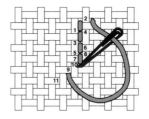

Plastic Canvas

Plastic canvas allows for three-dimensional stitchery projects to be constructed. Stitching on plastic canvas is easy to do, easy on the eyes, and easy on the pocketbook, too.

Basic Supplies

Plastic Canvas: Canvas is most widely available by the sheet. Stitch all the pieces of a project on the same brand of plastic canvas to ensure that the meshes will match when you join them together.

Plastic canvas comes in several counts or mesh sizes (number of stitches to the inch) and numerous sizes of sheets. Specialty sizes and shapes such as circles are also available. Most canvas is clear, although up to 24 colors are available. Colored canvas is used when parts of the project remain unstitched. Seven-count canvas comes in four weights—standard; a thinner flexible weight; a stiffer, rigid weight; and a softer weight made especially for bending and curved projects. Designs can be stitched on any mesh count—the resulting size of the project is the only thing that will be affected. The smaller the count number, the larger the project will be, since the count number refers to the number of stitches per inch. Therefore, seven-count has seven stitches per inch, while 14-count has 14. A 14-count project will be half the size of a seven-count project.

Needles: Needle size is determined by the count size of the plastic canvas you are using. Patterns generally call for a #18 needle for stitching on 7-count plastic canvas, a #16 or #18 for 10-count canvas, and a #22 or #24 for stitching on 14-count plastic canvas.

Yarns: A wide variety of yarns may be used. The most common is worsted weight (or 4-ply). Acrylic yarns are less expensive and washable; wool may also be used. Several companies produce specialty yarns for plastic canvas work. These cover the canvas well and will not "pill" as some acrylics do. Sport weight yarn (or 3-ply) and embroidery floss are often used on 10-count canvas. Use 12 strands or double the floss thickness for 10-count canvas and 6 strands for stitching on 14-count canvas.

Preparing to Stitch

Cut your yarn to a 36-inch length. Begin by holding the yarn end behind the fabric until secured or covered over with two or three stitches. To end a length, weave or run the yarn under several stitches on the back side. Cut the end close to the canvas. Decorative stitches will add interest and texture to your project. As in cross-stitch, if your yarn begins to twist, drop the needle and allow the yarn to untwist. It is important to the final appearance of the project to keep an even tension when pulling your stitches through so that all of your stitches have a uniform look. Do not pull your stitches too tight. Also do not carry one color yarn across too many rows of another color on the back—the carried color may show through to the front of your project. Do not stitch the outer edge of the canvas until the other stitching is complete. If the project is a single piece of canvas, overcast the outer edge with the color specified. If there are two or more pieces, follow the pattern instructions for assembly.

Cleaning

If projects are stitched with acrylic yarn, they may be washed by hand using warm or cool water and a mild detergent. Place on a terry cloth towel to air dry. Do not place in a dryer or dry clean.

The following stitches are used in this book:

*The **Hardanger stitch** is worked by skipping rows between the top and bottom of the stitch. Your needle comes up at 1 and all odd-numbered holes and goes down at 2 and all even-numbered holes.*

*The **overcast stitch** is used to finish edges; it may be worked in either direction. The needle goes down at the numbered holes, and the yarn wraps over the edge of the canvas. Make sure to cover the canvas completely—you may go through the same hole two or more times*

Wearables

You'll find fabric painting to be fast, easy, and fun. With the latest development in fabric paints, using basic dimensional paints is almost as easy as writing with a ballpoint pen. Some of the painting projects will require a brush—we'll tell you what type of brush you'll need in the project's materials list.

Protecting Your Project
We have used waxed paper ironed to the inside of the shirt. This prevents paint from bleeding through and makes it easier to transport a project with wet paint. You can also use a shirt board or you can make your own by cutting corrugated cardboard into the shape of a flattened T-shirt about ½ inch smaller than the shirt you'll be using. Cover it with wax paper and insert it into the item you'll be working on. Make sure the waxed side is under the surface you want to paint.

Paints
Each of the projects will specify the type of paints required. Only dimensional and embellished paints, which are especially formulated to use on fabric, are used. For specific instructions for each paint, follow the instructions on the packaging or bottle.

Basic Guidelines for Wearables
• Prewash fabric and wearables without using any fabric softeners. Softeners prevent the paint from bonding completely with the fibers. Press out any wrinkles.

• If you're right-handed, work on your project from the upper left-hand corner to the lower right-hand corner. Paint all colors as you go. This will prevent you from accidentally smearing the paint with your elbow or hand.

• When using dimensional paints, pick up the tube of paint with the cap on and shake the paint down into the tip to remove any air bubbles each time you use a color. Place a paint bottle down on its side between uses.

• Hold your dimensional paint bottle like a ballpoint pen. Squeeze gently and work quickly and smoothly. Moving too slowly often results in a "bumpy" appearance.

• When using dimensional glitter paint, be sure to draw a line of paint that is thick enough to carry the glitter.

• Allow paints to dry at least 6 to 8 hours before touching. Allow 36 to 48 hours for paint to be completely cured before wearing.

Caring For Your Wearable
Hand or machine wash in lukewarm water—not cold!!—in delicate/knit cycle. Cold water will crack the paint. Tumble dry on low for a few minutes to remove wrinkles, then remove and lay flat to dry. Do not wash using Woolite or other delicate care wash products.

Sewing

The excitement of making your own holiday crafts sometimes gets in the way of your preparation. Before plunging into your chosen project, check to make sure you have all the materials needed. Being prepared will make your sewing easier and more fun. Most of the items you need will probably be on hand already.

Scissors: two styles are needed, one about eight to ten inches long with bent handle for cutting fabric. This style of scissors allows you to cut through the fabric while the fabric lays flat. These shears should be sharp and used only for fabric. The second style of scissors is smaller, about six inches, with sharp points. You will need this style for smaller projects and close areas.

Straight Pins: nonrusting dressmaker pins are best to use. They will not leave rust marks on your fabric if they come in contact with dampness or glue.

Tape Measure: should be plastic coated so that it will not stretch and can be wiped off if it comes in contact with paint or glue.

Ironing Board and Steam Iron: Be sure your ironing board is well padded and has a clean covering. Sometimes you do more sewing with the iron than you do with the sewing machine. Keeping your fabrics, seams, and hems pressed cuts down on stitches and valuable time. A steam or dry iron is best. It is important to press your fabric to achieve a professional look. The iron is also used to adhere the fusible interfacing. Keep the bottom of your iron clean and free of any substance that could mark your fabric. The steam iron may be used directly on most fabrics with no shine. Test a small piece of the fabric first. If it causes a shine on the right side, try the reverse side.

Thread: Have mercerized sewing thread in the colors needed for each project you have chosen. Proper shade and strength (about a 50 weight) of thread avoids having the stitching show more than is necessary and the item will have a finished look.

HeatNBond Interfacing: This is a lightweight fusible iron-on adhesive. HeatNBond is placed paper side up on wrong side of material. Place iron on paper side of adhesive and press for one to three seconds. Allow fabric to cool. Design can then be drawn or traced onto the paper side and cut out. Remove the paper and place the material right side up in desired position on project and iron for three to five seconds.

Sewing Machine: Neat, even stitches are achieved in a very few minutes with a sewing machine and helps you complete your project with ease. If desired, you may machine stitch a zigzag stitch around the attached fusible adhesive pieces to secure the edges.

Work Surface: your sewing surface should be a comfortable height for sitting and roomy enough to lay out your projects. Keep it clean and free of other crafting materials that could accidently spill or soil your fabric.

Jewelry Making

Although the jewelry in this book looks sophisticated, most is made by gluing. Jewelry findings is a term for a variety of ready-made metal components used as attachments and fastenings to assemble jewelry. They are usually made of inexpensive metal. Findings include pin backs, earring findings, barrel clasps, jump rings, and beading wire—for our projects you will need pin backs and earring findings. All of these are found in your local craft or hobby store.

A Word About Glue

Glue can be a sticky subject when you don't use the right one for the job. There are many different glues on the craft market today, each formulated for a different crafting purpose. The following are ones you should be familiar with:

White Glue: This may be used as an all-purpose glue—it dries clear and flexible. It is often referred to as craft glue or tacky glue. Tacky on contact, it allows you to put two items together without a lot of set up time required. Use for most projects, especially ones involving wood, plastics, some fabrics, and cardboard.

Thin-Bodied Glues: Use these glues when your project requires a smooth, thin layer of glue. Thin-bodied glues work well on some fabrics and papers.

Fabric Glue: This type of glue is made to bond with fabric fibers and withstand repeated washing. Use this kind of glue for attaching rhinestones and/or other charms to fabric projects. Some glues require heat-setting. Check the bottle for complete instructions.

Hot Melt Glue: Formed into cylindrical sticks, this glue is inserted into a hot temperature glue gun and heated to liquid state. Depending on the type of glue gun used, the glue is forced out through the gun's nozzle by either pushing on the end of the glue stick or squeezing a trigger. Use clear glue sticks for projects using wood, fabrics, most plastics, ceramics, and cardboard. When using any glue gun, be careful of the nozzle and the freshly applied glue—it is very hot! Apply glue to the piece being attached. Work with small areas at a time so that the glue doesn't set before being pressed into place.

Low Melt Glue: This is similar to hot melt glues in that it is formed into sticks and requires a glue gun to be used. Low melt glues are used for projects that would be damaged by heat. Examples include foam, balloons, and metallic ribbons. Low melt glue sticks are oval-shaped and can only be used in a low temperature glue gun.

Decorative Wood Painting

Paints

There are a wide variety of paint brands to choose from. Acrylic paints are available at your local arts and crafts stores in a wide variety of brands. Mix and match your favorite colors to paint the projects in this book. These projects will work with any acrylic paint brands.

Acrylic paint dries in minutes and allows projects to be completed in no time at all. Clean hands and brushes with soap and water.

Some projects may require a medium that is not acrylic or water based. These require mineral spirits to clean up. Always check the manufacturer's label before working with a product so you have the proper supplies.

Finishes

Choose from a wide variety of types and brands of varnishes to protect your finished project. Varnish is available in both spray or brush on.

Brush on water base varnishes dry in minutes and clean up with soap and water. Use over any acrylic paints. Don't use over paints or mediums requiring mineral spirits clean up.

Spray varnishes can be used over any type of paint or medium. For projects with a pure white surface, choose a nonyellowing varnish. The slight yellowing of some varnishes can actually enhance for a richer look. Varnishes are available in matte, satin, or gloss finishes. Choose the shine you prefer.

Brushes and Paint Supplies

Foam (sponge) brushes work great to seal, basecoat, and varnish wood. Clean foam brushes with soap and water when using acrylic paints and mediums. For paints or mediums that require mineral spirits to clean up, you will have to throw the disposable brush away.

Synthetic brushes work well with acrylic paints for details and designs. You will use a liner brush for thin lines and details. A script brush is needed for extra long lines. Round brushes fill in round areas, stroke work, and broad lines. An angle brush is used to fill in large areas, float, or side-load color. A large flat brush is used to apply basecoat and varnish. Small flat brushes are for stroke work and basecoating small areas.

Wood Preparation

Properly preparing your wood piece can make all the difference in the outcome. Having a smooth surface to work on will allow you to complete the project quickly and easily. Once the wood is prepared, you are ready to proceed with a basecoat, stain, or finish, according to the project instructions. Some finishes, such as crackling, will recommend not sealing the wood. Always read instructions completely before starting.

Supplies you will need to prepare the wood: sand paper (#200) for removing roughness; tack cloth, which is a sticky resin treated cheese cloth, to remove dust after sanding; a wood sealer to seal wood and prevent warping; and a foam or one-inch flat brush to apply sealer.

Dots

Perfect round dots can be made with any round implement. The size of the implement determines the size of the dot. You can use the wooden end of a brush, a stylus tip, a pencil tip, or the eraser end of pencil (with an unused eraser).

Use undiluted paint for thick dots or dilute paint with 50 percent water for smooth dots. Dip the tip into paint and then onto the surface. For uniform dots, you must redip in paint for each dot. For graduated dots, continue dotting with same paint load. Clean tip on paper towel after each group and reload.

To create hearts, place two dots of the same size next to each other. Then drag paint from each dot down to meet in bottom of heart.

Floating Color

This technique is also called side loading. It is used to shade or highlight the edge of an object. Floated color is a gradual blend of color to water.

1 Moisten an angle brush with water. Blot excess water from brush, setting bristles on paper towel until shine of water disappears.

2 Dip the long corner of angle brush into paint. Load paint sparingly. Carefully stroke brush on palette until color blends halfway across the brush. If the paint blends all the way to short side, clean and load again. For thicker paint, dilute first with 50 percent water.

3 Hold the brush at a 45 degree angle, and using a light touch, apply color to designated area.

Making a Multiloop Bow

There are many ways to make bows, and the more you make, the easier it becomes. Follow the instructions, and before long you will be a pro.

To make your bows more professional, here are two ways to cut ribbon ends:

To V cut ribbon, gently fold the ribbon ends in half lengthwise. Cut from the outside edge up a half inch toward the fold.

To angle-cut ribbon, cut the ends at an angle in either direction.

1 Crimp the ribbon between thumb and forefinger at the desired streamer length, with the streamer hanging down. Make an equal number of loops on each side of your thumb by crimping each individually while you guide the ribbon into a loop in a circular direction. Crimp each new loop next to the previous one, rather than on top. Secure the loops in the center with wire twisted tightly on the back, leaving the second streamer pointing up.

2 While holding the bow in the same position, roll three inches of that streamer toward you over your thumb, making a small center loop as a knot. If the ribbon has a right and wrong side, twist the loop right side out and catch the loop under your thumb. The streamer will again be pointing up. Bring one end of wire from the back over that streamer beside the knot and to the back again. Twist the wires again. Bring the streamers together beneath the bow and V or angle-cut the ends at different lengths.

Molly Mop Bunny

Molly is ready for Easter with her
decorated straw hat and big pink bow.
Won't you place her in your home?

What You'll Need

24-inch cotton mop
(No. 24)

10-inch section white
nylon

Fiberfill

Craft stick

Sewing needle (long)
and white thread

2-temp glue gun,
glue sticks

2 yellow animal eyes,
18mm each

¾-inch pink pom-pom

Pink pastel chalk

Cotton ball

8 × 12-inch piece white
fun foam

Scissors

10-inch straw hat

12 × 20-inch jumbo
creative twist

3 yards colonial rose
creped ribbon,
1½ inches wide

12 to 24 small rose
ribbon roses

10 yards rose double-face
satin ribbon, ⅛ inch wide

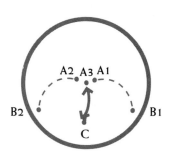

1 Tie an overhand knot in one end of nylon section; reverse. Stuff nylon tube with two handfuls of fiberfill. Insert craft stick in opening and half way into center of head stuffing. Close head by wrapping thread around nylon and stick, just below stuffing. Tie off thread.

2 To make first cheek, start thread from back of neck; come out at A1. Sew shallow stitch line two inches long, curving down the last few stitches to B1. Bring needle through head coming out at A1; pull taut, back to B1, then back to A1.

3 Move needle over ½ inch to form A2, pull taut, stitch back to A1, and repeat three times. To make second cheek, follow instructions for first cheek, substituting A2 and B2 for A1 and B1 (do not start at back of neck this time).

4 To form mouth, go under from A2 coming out halfway between A1 and A2, creating A3. Insert needle into point C, scoop under stuffing to A3; repeat this three to four times, pulling taut. Secure by going back to base of neck, and knot off. Cut off shank of eyes, and glue just above cheek line. Glue ¾-inch pink pom-pom for nose. Add blush to cheeks with cotton ball and pink chalk.

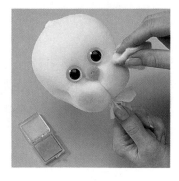

5 Glue front side of craft stick (on head) to mop center. Use one loose mop strand to wind around stick and mop neck. Tie with double knot.

6 Separate 18 mop strands from each side for arms. Braid, tie off, and trim.

7 Fold eight loose strands in half and glue (four front and four back) to cover mop center and stick.

8 Let strands drape loose. Glue strands from skirt to cover balance of mop center, if needed. Tie some strands into knots. For a fuller skirt look, separate mop ends.

9 Cut out two ears from white fun foam. (See pattern for ear on page 53. Enlarge on copy machine by 20 percent.) Dust inside of ears with pink pastel chalk. Glue ears to each side of head.

10 Using arm trimmings and loose mop strands, glue hair to front half of hat (fill in solid, so no space is left from hat brim to head). Glue hat to bunny head; hold until glue is set.

11 Cut 12 inches of creped ribbon. Hand gather and glue apron (untwisted creative twist) to center of ribbon. Glue apron around mop (just under arm braids). Overlap apron in back and trim apron and ribbon if necesary.

12 Glue creped ribbon around hat (overlap ends ½ inch). Make three simple two-loop bows of creped ribbon. Glue one bow to back of waistband. Glue one bow to side of hat, to cover hatband ends. Glue last bow under the bunny's chin.

13 Using narrow coordinating ribbon and ribbon roses, randomly tie accents to skirt and around wrists. For hanger, attach a mop strand around neck and through hat; tie in a double knot on back side of hat.

Dove's Home

Satin ribbon roses outline this lovely painted
birdhouse. The saucy bird perched on top is
decked out in its Easter finery!

What You'll Need

Wood birdhouse

1½ × ⅛-inch wood heart

Acrylic paint: wisteria and gp purple

Flat paintbrush

8 white looped pearl sprays

Low-temp glue gun, glue sticks

1½ yards white satin roses on ribbon (36 roses)

Black permanent marker

3 white lace leaves, 2½ inches each

3-inch white mushroom dove

1 Paint roof and base of birdhouse with gp purple. Paint main frame with wisteria. Paint wood heart gp purple. Allow to dry. Cut two small loops from one of the pearl sprays. Glue ends of loop to front top of painted heart.

2 Cut ribbon from one satin rose. Glue rose over ends of pearl spray on heart. Write welcome on front of heart with permanent marker. Set heart to side.

3 Starting at a back corner of birdhouse base, glue satin rose to outside edge of base with glue gun. Continue around edge until entire base is lined with satin roses. Ribbon between roses should be loose, not tight. Allow three roses per side of base. Repeat process for outside edge of roof. Allow for a rose per corner, three per side, and five for the front and back.

4 Trim stems of pearl sprays to ¼ inch (¼ inch of tape is needed to secure loops). Apply a small puddle of glue to birdhouse roof (on one side of roof toward back). Working quickly, arrange pearl sprays in a circular pattern.

5 Trim stem wire from lace leaves. Apply a small amount of glue to back of lace leaves and attach over pearl sprays.

6 Trim ribbon from remaining roses. Glue roses to neckline of dove. Apply a small amount of glue to bottom of dove. Place dove at center of pearl spray and lace leaves. Place welcome heart onto bird perch.

Pink Lace Bunny

Flopsy and Mopsy have nothing on this
adorable soft sculpture bunny. She's all dressed
up and just waiting for someone to love her!

What You'll Need

14-inch muslin bunny

1 yard double-pleated pink ribbon with lace

Scissors

21 × 6-inch piece small print fabric

Sewing needle and thread

6-inch round doily

Tacky glue

2-inch pink bow with pearl

12-inch length pink satin ribbon, 1/16 inch wide

Carrot button

1 Cut double-pleated ribbon into five pieces: one 21 inches, two 3 1/2 inches, and two 4 inches. Glue 21-inch piece to bottom edge of right side of printed fabric. Apply a thin line of glue 1/4 inch above bottom edge of printed fabric and press ribbon into glue. Allow glue to set.

2 Apply a thin line of glue to one side edge of fabric. Fold fabric over to 10 1/2 × 6 inches. Press opposite fabric edge into glue. Dress is wrong side out. Let dry.

3 Cut two-inch arm slits at top center of dress. One cut will make both (two) arm slits. Turn dress right side out.

4 Place dress on doll. Working back to front, fold top edge of dress over 1/4 inch and gather neckline with running stitch. Pull thread through to back (starting point) and knot off.

5 Cut two-inch slit in from doily edge. Starting in back of doily, cut a center opening 1 1/2 inches in diameter.

6 Place doily on bunny's neck with slit in back. Glue back of doily to bunny by slightly overlapping edges. Glue bow over the overlapping ends.

7 Thread pink ribbon through shank on back side of carrot button. Knot carrot to ribbon at center of ribbon. Place carrot necklace around bunny's neck and knot off ribbon in back.

8 Glue 3 1/2 inches of double-pleated ribbon to wrist of bunny. Join ends of ribbon in back. Repeat with second piece of 3 1/2 inch length of ribbon for other wrist. Glue four-inch double-pleated ribbon to ankle of bunny. Join ends in back. Repeat with second piece of ribbon for other ankle.

Watering Can Centerpiece

Brighten up your Easter brunch with this
whimsical bunny stuck in a watering can.
You'll want to keep this bunny out year-round!

What You'll Need

10-inch violet watering can

Dry floral foam block

Serrated knife
(or craft knife)

Tacky glue

Pink silk baby's breath bush

Wire cutters

11-inch muslin bunny

White chenille stem

2 silk rosewood delphini-
ums

1 purple silk delphinium

2 pink silk lilacs

1 purple silk lilac stem

1 purple silk crocus

Glass egg ornament set

16-inch pink paper-cov-
ered floral wire

Small pink bow

1 Cut floral foam with serrated knife to fit inside of watering can.

2 Apply several lines of tacky glue to inside bottom of watering can. Insert floral block into watering can and press down to secure.

3 Trim excess wire from baby's breath with wire cutters. Leave one inch of wire stem. Place watering can so handle is to left side and spout is to the right. Insert baby's breath into floral block. Bend baby's breath out slightly.

4 Bend bunny legs up toward bunny back. Wrap chenille stem around bunny to secure it in this position. Stick bunny into center of baby's breath with bunny facing front. Arrange legs and arms. Legs should stick out back. Spread bunny's arms out.

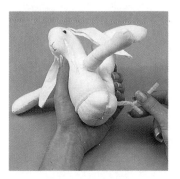

5 Insert delphiniums to left of bunny. Insert lilacs to right of bunny. Insert crocus in front of bunny's right arm. String glass egg ornaments on covered wire. Wrap wire ends around bunny's arms. Glue bow to bunny's neck with tacky glue.

Ladybug Barrette

A flower and ribbon create a fetching hairpiece
to wear in the Easter parade! Ladybugs, good
luck signs, finish this fun barrette.

What You'll Need

2⅜-inch steel bow barrette

7 inches white double-
ruffle ribbon, #5

Sewing needle
and white thread

Tacky glue

1 small yellow silk flower

3 ladybug picks

Wire cutters

1 Fold in ¼ inch of raw ends of ruffled ribbon. Finger press folds.

2 Sew a running stitch down middle of ribbon. Pull gather to measure 3⅓ inches and knot off. Apply a thin line of tacky glue down middle of wrong side of ribbon (follow along running stitch). Press ribbon onto barrette with glue side down. Hold firm until glue sets.

3 Trim back of flower by removing any wire or plastic stem from flower. Glue flower to center of barrette with tacky glue.

4 Cut wire from bottoms of ladybug picks. Glue a ladybug to each end of ribbon and one ladybug on top of flower.

Welcome Spring Door Swag

Greet visitors with the natural beauty of spring

in this lovely door swag!

What You'll Need

5 × 1½-inch green foam disc

18-gauge wire

Spanish moss

Greening pins (craft pins)

Natural twig branches, approx. 28 inches long

Tacky glue

3 silk sprays silk English ivy foliage

Preserved springerii

1 spray silk forsythia, divided

3 dark pink stems silk almond blossoms

8 pink silk crocus blossoms

1 purple silk violet cluster

3 silk Boston fern fronds

1⅔ yards yellow paper twist, 3 inches wide

28-gauge wire

1 Using 12-inch length of 18-gauge wire, fold in half and twist to form a one-inch loop. To form hanger push ends of wire through foam disc. Twist ends of wire together on opposite side (front) of disc. Cover front with Spanish moss and secure with greening pins.

2 Dip all stems into glue before inserting into foam. Insert approximately 18 twig branches into bottom. The longest branch should be about 28 inches. Radiate eight- to ten-inch branches out each side.

3 Insert approximately 18 twig branches, the longest about 14 inches, into the top.

4 Insert stems of English ivy, allowing some to cascade over longer twig branches. Arrange some sprigs of ivy out to the sides and one sprig upward over top branches. Fill around outer edge with springerii. Place the three Boston fern fronds. Direct one to the left of center and one to the right of center. Allow the third to drop down from the right.

5 Divide forsythia spray so that you have six sprigs. Direct the longest of the three lower sprigs to fall down over the lower twigs. Place lower three sprigs to left side and the three shorter sprigs on top pointing to the right.

6 Cut a 30-inch length of paper twist and untwist it. Arrange vertically on the arrangement. Secure ribbon with greening pin into foam and glue to branches in several places. Using rest of paper ribbon, fold into bow shape measuring eight inches in diameter, with seven-inch streamers. Wire bow together in center with 28-gauge wire. Trim excess wire. Slip greening pin through bow wire and insert into foam over twig branches.

7 Using a clock as a guide, insert almond blossoms between 9 and 11 o'clock and between 4 and 6 o'clock. Insert stems of crocus around center of arrangement and one blossom in center above bow. Add the violets across bow.

Fresh from the Garden

Indulge yourself with fresh carrots any time
of the year! These fun carrots make a great
addition to a gift basket or a table centerpiece.

What You'll Need

½ yard orange fabric
(for 20 carrots)

Scrap paper and pencil

Scissors

Pins

Sewing machine

Orange thread

Fiberfill

Stuffing stick (chopstick, unsharpened pencil, etc.)

12 × 3-inch piece heavy cardboard

Skeins of light, medium, and dark green yarn

Sewing needle

1 Trace several carrot patterns (on page 26) onto scrap paper. Cut out patterns from paper. Fold orange fabric twice. Pin paper carrot patterns and cut carrots out of fabric.

2 Fold fabric carrot in half lengthwise. Sew side seam with sewing machine threaded with orange thread. Repeat this step for remaining carrots. Vary seam allowance using ⅛, ¼, and ⅜ inches. Use large, medium, and small carrot patterns with different seam allowances for different size carrots.

3 Trim excess fabric from side seam. Clip tip of fabric carrot. Turn carrot right side out. Stuff carrot with fiberfill—use small amounts of fiberfill at a time. Use chopstick or unsharpened pencil to push fiberfill into carrot. Stuff carrot firmly until ¾ full.

4 Wrap yarns (all three colors at the same time) around yarn template (cardboard). Cut yarn off template from one end. Gather 12 to 20 strands. Holding all strands, tie a knot in center of strands, pulling yarn tightly. For variety in carrot tops, vary the number of strands used for each carrot top. Repeat this step for each carrot.

5 Fold unfinished edge of top of carrot down ½ inch. Starting at seam, sew a running stitch around top of fabric carrot. Insert a carrot top into stuffed carrot cavity. Pull running stitch tight. Knot off. Repeat this step for remaining carrots. Trim carrot top yarn if desired.

6 Assemble carrots in a decorative basket with gardening tools, gloves, seed packets, and other gardening equipment for a decorative centerpiece.

LARGE CARROT

MEDIUM CARROT

SMALL CARROT

Easter Gift Basket

Lovely colorful flowers burst

from an ivy-laden basket—

the joy of springtime!

What You'll Need

Woven basket with handle

1 brick dry floral foam

Serrated knife

18-gauge floral wire

Wire cutters

Sheet moss

Greening pins

Green floral tape

Tacky glue

5 sprays silk English ivy

3 purple silk irises

5 dark pink silk tulips

5 yellow silk daffodils

1 silk violet cluster

2 white sprays small silk blossoms

Preserved asparagus fern

2 yards yellow satin ribbon, 1½ inches wide

28-gauge wire

1 Cut foam to fit into basket. Fill basket with all pieces so that foam fits snugly. Wire across top of foam using 18-gauge wire to secure.

2 Cover foam with moss and secure with greening pins.

3 Place long strand of ivy over basket handle, securing with floral tape at random places. If ivy is not long enough, tape a few stems together with floral tape to form a longer piece. Cut ivy into six- to eight-inch sprigs and place into foam around edge of basket, and place several in center of basket. (Note: Dip all stems into glue before inserting into foam.)

4 Place irises into arrangement. First stem is placed behind the handle to left of center, with top of blossom about six inches above handle. Second iris is placed behind the handle to the left of first iris, and blossom is a bit taller than handle. Third iris is placed in front of the handle between the two back irises.

5 Four tulips are placed in front of the handle at staggered heights and the tallest tulip is placed behind the handle to the right of the tall iris, but even in height with the front iris.

6 Three daffodils cascade down the right front of the arrangement and two fill in the back.

7 Fill in the arrangement with violet cluster beneath the center tulip and sprigs of white silk blossoms and preserved asparagus fern.

8 Using yellow satin ribbon, make a six-loop bow (see page 10). eight inches in diameter with six-inch streamers. Use a length of 28-gauge wire to secure bow. Slip greening pin through bow wire and insert into arrangement beneath the lowest daffodil on right side.

Headed for the Garden

This soft sculptured bunny looks all ready

to garden—but she'll hold all your

important notes on the refrigerator!

What You'll Need

3-inch muslin bunny

6 × 2-inch piece of fabric

6-inch length flat lace

Scissors

Sewing machine
and thread

Iron

Sewing needle

Tacky glue

Miniature gardening tool

Miniature watering can

Magnet

1 Sew lace to bottom edge of fabric. Iron lace flat if needed. Fold dress in half and sew back seam with ⅛-inch seam allowance. Cut one-inch arm slit at center top of dress (both arm slits will be cut at same time because fabric is folded). Turn dress right side out.

2 Working from back to front, fold arm slit sides in ¼ inch and neckline down ¼ inch. Finger press folds. With needle and thread and using a running stitch, start in the middle of the back and continue through to front neckline. Place dress on bunny; be sure seam is in back. Continue sewing with running stitch to starting place. Gather neckline firmly. Knot off.

3 Tack-stitch gardening tool to one bunny arm. Tack-stitch watering can to other arm.

4 Lift dress and dab a small amount of glue on bunny back. Lower dress and press dress into glue. Glue magnet to back of bunny.

Funny Bunny Jewelry

Add a festive touch

to your spring wardrobe

with this amusing jewelry!

What You'll Need

Wood girl peg doll shape (makes 2 pins)

Saw-band, scroll, or back hand saw

Fine grain sanding paper

Paper clay modeling compound

Acrylic paint: white, Lisa pink, tangerine, copen blue

Flat paintbrush

Pink paint marker

Black permanent marker

4 miniature plastic eggs (pink, purple, blue, yellow)

Several strands green raffia

Cement glue

Miniature basket

2 white pom-poms, ¼ inch each

2 pin backs, 1 inch each

2 wood balls, ½ inch each

2 cupped earring posts with backs

Scissors

2 eye pins, 25mm each

2 fishhook earring findings, 20mm each

Needlenose pliers

Note: Wash and dry hands well before using modeling compound. Work quickly and only on one piece at a time. When base coating, remember to paint modeling compound. If modeling compound comes loose, just glue piece to wood with tacky glue. When dry, the modeling compound feels firm, flexible, and lightweight.

1 Cut peg doll in half with saw. Be very careful to protect your fingers and eyes. Sand any rough edges. To make an ear, pinch a small piece of modeling compound from package. Roll into a ball that measures about ½ inch in diameter.

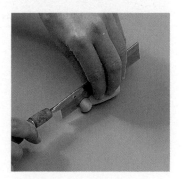

2 Roll modeling compound between fingers. Start to form into cone shape that measures about one inch. Flatten top and bottom of cone.

3 Press small point end of ear to top of peg doll head overlapping to back of doll peg. Modeling compound will adhere to raw wood. Make second ear and attach to peg doll body.

4 To make feet, form same shape as ear. Press points into bottom of doll overlapping to back.

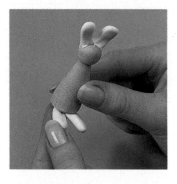

5 To form arms, form same shape as ear. Attach arm to wood body with point toward neck. Gently press arm to wood. Repeat process for second arm. Repeat steps 2 through 5 for second bunny.

6 Pinch a small pea size piece of modeling compound from package. Roll into small carrot shape. Cut one strand of green raffia into several one-inch pieces. Insert raffia into top of carrot. Allow modeling compound to dry 24 hours.

7 Glue pin backs to back of each peg doll half. Allow glue to set. Paint entire bunny pin white. Allow to dry. Apply second coat if needed. Using pink paint marker, dot foot pads on feet. Draw small heart nose. Color inside of ear.

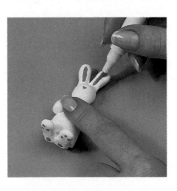

8 For one bunny only, use black permanent marker to draw a short line down from point of heart nose to complete mouth. For both bunnies, squeeze a small amount of copen blue

both bunnies, dip stylus into paint and dot two eyes to each side of face just above nose. Redip stylus into paint for each eye (see page 9).

9 For other bunny (without black line for mouth), float two Lisa pink cheeks on face (see page 10). Squeeze a small puddle of Lisa pink paint onto scrap paper. Wet a flat paintbrush with water. Remove excess water with paper towel (water should not drip from brush). Dip one corner of paintbrush into paint. Stroke brush back and forth on clean scrap paper. When paint begins to blend from dark to light on scrap paper, float or stroke two cheeks on wood body. Touch brush flat to wood and stroke with a slight curve or upside down U shape.

10 To finish, glue three eggs into miniature basket. Glue basket to bunny pin with black line on face. Glue last egg to top of one foot. Paint carrot tangerine. Allow to dry. Glue carrot to other bunny's arm. Glue a pom-pom to bottom back of each pin.

11 For bunny earrings: Glue wood balls to cupped earring posts with cement glue. Allow glue to set. To make ear, pinch a small piece of modeling compound from package. Roll into a ball that measures about 3/8 inch in diameter. Using thumb and forefinger, roll modeling compound between fingers. Form into cone shape that measures about one inch. Flatten top and bottom of cone shape. Ear will look like the top of an exclamation point.

12 Press small point end of ear to top of wood ball overlapping to back of wood ball at earring post (see step 3 photo). Modeling compound will adhere to raw wood. Make second ear and attach to wood ball. Repeat process for second earring. Allow modeling compound to dry 24 hours.

13 Base coat bunny earrings with white paint. Allow to dry. Using pink paint pen, draw heart nose on bunny face. Color inside of ears. With black permanent marker, draw short straight line on front of face below heart nose.

14 Float two Lisa pink cheeks to face. See step 9 instructions and photo.

15 For carrot earrings: To make a carrot, pinch a small piece of modeling compound from package. Roll into a ball that measures about 5/8 inch in diameter. Roll modeling compound between fingers and form into cone shape that measures about one inch. Flatten top and bottom of cone shape. Repeat for other earring.

16 Cut strands of green raffia into one-inch pieces. Bunch six to eight cut pieces and insert into top of cone. Cut eye pin to measure 1/2 inch. Insert cut end of eye pin into top of carrot. Where eye pin is inserted will become back of earring. Allow modeling compound to dry 24 hours.

17 Paint carrot with tangerine paint. Attach fishhook earring to eye pin. Gently open fishhook with needlenoose pliers, place eye of pin in fishhook, and close fishhook with needlenose pliers.

Spring Mugs

What better way to brighten a rainy day

than with mugs decorated with

spring flowers and pastel colors!

What You'll Need

2 mugs (with vinyl weave inserts)

#24 tapestry needle

Embroidery floss: maroon, dark pink, medium pink, light pink, gold, dark yellow, medium yellow, light yellow, dark green, medium green, light green, light blue, dark blue, black

Scissors

1 Take mug apart and remove vinyl weave strip. Find center horizontally and vertically and mark with a pin or needle. Find center of chart by using arrows to determine where to begin stitching. Cross-stitch and backstitch with two of six strands of floss. Work cross-stitches first, then backstitch. For light blue strips, work just one leg of the cross-stitch in the direction indicated.

2 For second mug, insert daffodils in place of tulips. When stitching is completed, insert vinyl weave into mugs, placing seams next to handle. Snap insert into mug.

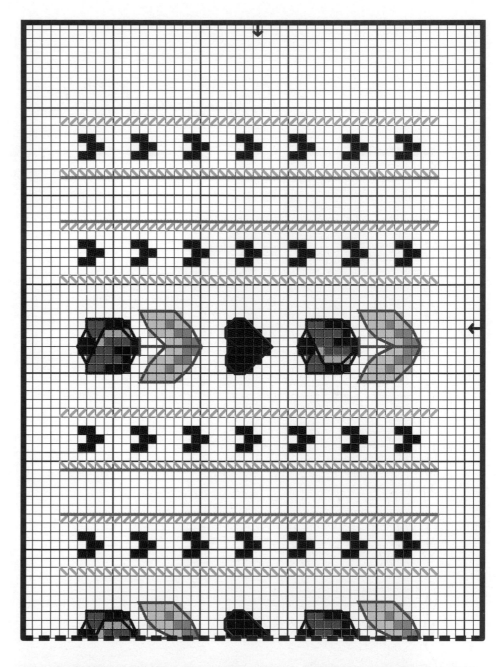

Maroon
Dark pink
Medium pink
Light pink
Dark green
Medium green
Light green
Dark blue
Light blue
Gold
Dark yellow
Medium yellow
Light yellow

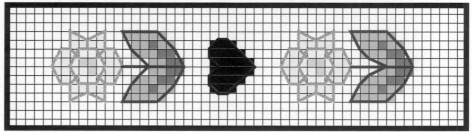

Flowers and Babies

Cute baby animals painted on a toddler romper

are the perfect accent for Easter morning.

What grandparent can resist this picture?

What You'll Need

- Infant bubble suit
- Freezer paper
- Iron
- Typing paper
- Iron-on transfer pens: black, green
- Waxed paper
- 8 × 10-inch square of netting
- Fine point fabric markers: green, blue, lavender, pink, black, brown, bullet-point gray
- Brush-on fabric paint: peach, lavender, light blue, green, sparkling gold, sparkling dusty-rose, sparkling aqua, sparkling white
- #2 and #4 flat paintbrushes
- Fine point permanent black marker

1 Prepare infant suit by washing and drying it. Don't use fabric softener; paints will not adhere to fabric. Turn suit inside out, and iron freezer paper to front and back. Turn right side out.

2 Trace flower patterns (on next pages) on regular typing paper with transfer pens. Trace all foliage with green and all other patterns (flowers, animals) with black. This helps with color placement when base painting. Cut four flower sections apart, position, and pin to outfit. Use medium iron to transfer, one section at a time (check before removing pattern).

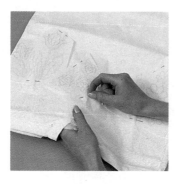

3 Cover animal patterns with waxed paper; secure with masking tape. Tape netting over pattern; trace outline and details with bullet-point gray marker. Remove tape. Tape netting to outfit (flowers should overlap bunny and lamb). Trace over pattern lines with bullet-point gray fabric marker (stop and start around flowers); remove netting.

4 Add fur (small slash marks) or straight outline on top of gray outline with assorted colors of fine point fabric markers. Add detail lines in flowers.

5 Base paint flowers and baby animals with soft paints and a brush in the following order: greenery, flowers, baby animals. Lightly brush pink into cheeks and ears of baby animals. Let dry. You can use finished picture as a guide for colors, or you can use your own color scheme.

Bunny Family & Chick Friends

Amuse your family and friends with these two
Easter families. With a few brush strokes, you'll
inspire many smiles!

What You'll Need

Wood doll kits
(Shelf Sweetie: Large/Tall,
Large/Short, Small/Short)

Scissors

Tacky glue

Acrylic paint: white, rouge,
copen blue, leaf green,
Bambi, black, Lisa pink, fire
red, bright yellow, rouge,
black, tangerine

3 wood skewers

2 flat paintbrushes

Paper towel and scrap
paper

Stylus

3 white pom-poms, ½ inch
each

2-inch square doily

12-inches pink double-face
satin ribbon, 1/16 inch wide

Hand drill with small
drill bit

3 wood skewers

3 yellow craft feathers

Black permanent marker

Bunny Family

1 Cut two wood craft sticks (included in doll kits) for each family member for ears. For poppa, cut sticks 3 inches long; for momma, cut sticks 2⅜ inches long; for baby, cut sticks 1½ inches long. Apply a thin line of tacky glue on one side of bottom raw edge of each stick. Attach craft sticks to back side of body. Be sure to place ears on correct body (poppa is largest, momma is middle, and baby is smallest). Allow glue to set.

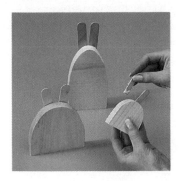

2 Base coat bodies with white paint. Allow to dry. Apply second coat of white. Let dry.

3 Dip a dry flat brush into Lisa pink paint. Wipe excess paint from brush on a paper towel. The brush is ready when only a hint of paint is seen on paper towel. Gently rub brush back and forth on ear to create a pink blush. Repeat on second ear.

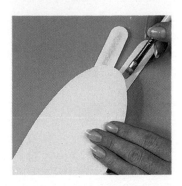

4 Dot a heart nose on body. Squeeze a small puddle of paint onto a piece of scrap paper (use black paint for poppa and baby, and Lisa pink for momma). Dip stylus into paint and place two dots of paint side by side (redip into paint after each dot). From center of two dots, pull paint down with stylus to form heart (practice on scrap paper first). Allow to dry. With permanent black marker, draw a short straight line from point of heart down to form mouth.

5 Dot two eyes on each body with stylus, being sure to redip after each dot. Use black paint for poppa and baby and copen blue paint for momma.

6 For poppa, squeeze a small puddle of Bambi paint onto a scrap piece of paper. Dip stylus into paint and dot freckles to face, spacing freckles to slightly above and below heart nose (do not redip after each dot).

7 For momma and baby, squeeze a small puddle of rouge paint onto scrap paper (see page 10). Wet a flat paintbrush with water. Remove excess water with paper towel (water should not drip from brush). Dip one corner of paintbrush into rouge paint. Stroke brush back and forth on clean scrap paper. When paint begins to blend from dark to light on scrap paper, float or stroke two cheeks on wood body. Touch brush flat to wood and stroke with a slight curve or upside down U shape. For momma bunny, use black marker to draw two half circles at bottom of black line to form a smile. Glue pom-poms to back of each body.

8 For momma, paint a carrot onto doily with tangerine (see finished shot for placement). Paint lines of leaf green at top of carrot. Allow paint to dry. Hand thread pink ribbon through top lace of doily. Place doily at ribbon center. Apply a thin line of glue to top wrong side of doily just below lace. Attach doily to front of momma. Tie ribbon in back and trim.

The Chick Family

1 Drill a small hole for hair, tail, and beak in each wood ball. (Poppa is largest ball, momma is medium, and peep is smallest ball.) Drill hair hole first, on the top middle of the ball. Using a measuring tape, measure 2 inches for poppa, 1½ inches for momma, and 1¼ inches for peep from hair hole to back for tail hole. Measure 1¼ inches for poppa, 1⅛ inches for momma, and ½ inch for peep from hair hole forward for beak hole. Drill holes at least ½ inch deep.

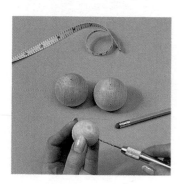

2 Base coat wood balls with bright yellow. Allow to dry. Apply a second and third coat of yellow if needed. Paint pointed ends of wood skewers with tangerine paint. Allow to dry. Trim two to ½ inch (poppa and momma), and one to ¼ inch (peep).

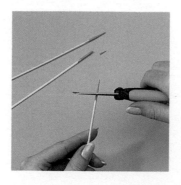

3 Place a small dab of glue inside each beak hole. Insert raw end of skewers into beak holes, being sure to place smallest skewer into smallest ball.

4 Cut two small pieces off each yellow feather. Apply a small amount of glue to ends of feathers. Inset feathers into hair and tail holes.

5 Squeeze a small amount of paint onto a piece of scrap paper. (Use rouge paint for poppa, fire red for momma, and Lisa pink for peep.) Dip the tip end of a paintbrush into paint. Dot two cheeks to each side of beak (redip after each cheek). Squeeze a small amount of black paint onto scrap piece of paper. (Use black for poppa and momma and copen blue for peep.) Dip stylus into paint and dot two eyes just above beak (redip for each eye).

Marvelous Miniature Baskets

These marvelous baskets are embellished with
colored thread and ribbon. What a great favor
to place at each setting for your Easter brunch!

What You'll Need

Two sheets ivory plastic canvas, 14 count each

#24 tapestry needle

Embroidery floss: pastel variegated, ecru

1 yard of each color satin ribbon (¼ inch wide): pink, blue, yellow, purple

Scissors

Craft knife

Craft glue

1 Cut pieces from plastic canvas as indicated on graph. Cut base 29 × 37 holes (this piece is unstitched). Cut two pieces 29 × 21 holes. Cut two pieces 37 × 21 holes. Handle is 13 × 59 holes.

2 Stitch sides and handle with six strands of variegated floss, using Hardanger stitch (see page 6). Take care not to carry floss across blank areas behind design.

3 Cut slits in plastic grid where indicated in pattern, using craft knife. Be careful not to slice floss.

4 Weave ribbon through slits, coming up after stitching and going back down before next group of stitching, attaching sides. Weave ribbon through a long side, a short side, a long side, and then a short side. Glue ribbon end on back of basket.

5 Whipstitch bottom to sides with six strands of ecru floss. Whipstitch handle to sides, matching rows as indicated by arrows. Using overcast stitch (see page 6), finish all raw edges.

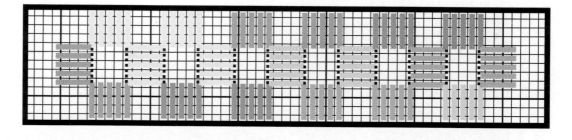

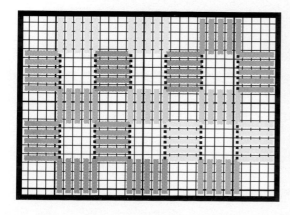

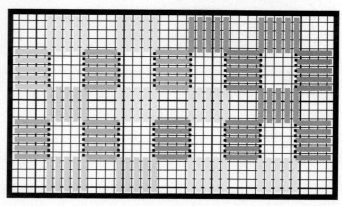

Garden Glories T-Shirt

A simple T-shirt becomes an elegant fashion

statement with a handpainted flower design.

Add a little glitter for some sparkle!

What You'll Need

T-shirt

Freezer paper

Iron

Iron-on transfer pens: black, green

Fabric markers: green, blue, lavender, red, brown

Spray bottle

Fabric paint: yellow, raspberry, purple, turquoise, green, desert rose, sunshine, red dazzle, blue daze, jade glow, gold, rose frost, ultra blue, jade stone

#2 and #6 flat paintbrushes

Fabric glitter: aurora dust, aurora sprinkle

1 Prepare shirt by prewashing garment. Don't use fabric softener; paint will not adhere to fabric. Turn inside out, and iron freezer paper to front. Turn right side out.

2 Trace flower pattern on next page (heavy black lines only) on regular typing paper with transfer pens. Trace all foliage with green and all flowers with black. This helps with color placement when base painting. Position and pin pattern to shirt. Use medium iron to transfer (check before removing pattern).

3 Trace all transferred outlines with assorted colors of fabric markers (set your own color scheme or use finished picture as a guide). Add detail lines in flowers.

4 Spray shirt with water until it is very damp, but not soaking. Using fabric paint at regular consistency, brush color on pattern starting with center (do not fill in solid); use paint sparingly. Bleeding will take up to 15 to 20 minutes and may favor one direction. If you wish to stop bleeding, use a handheld hair dryer. Colors will be lighter when they are dry, especially if you use a colored shirt, so do not water color down too much.

5 When dry, heat set following manufacturer's instructions. Accent design with fabric paint directly from bottle. Do not try to follow outline; add dimension and cover-up by creating a new outline.

6 Lightly sprinkle wet outline with fabric glitter (a little goes a long way). Let dry. Shake off excess glitter on newspaper (save for next project); remove freezer paper.

Hip-Hop the Easter Bunny

Place Hip-Hop where he

can greet your Easter visitors.

He's sure to delight everyone!

What You'll Need

Wood bunny kit

Sandpaper and tack cloth

Gesso

1-inch flat paintbrush

Scissors

4 × 6-inch piece white fun foam

Pink and lavender pastel chalk

Cotton balls

2-temp glue gun, glue sticks

2 split wood eggs, 1½ inches each

Clear acrylic spray

2 green animal eyes, 16mm each

½-inch glitter pink pom-pom

2-inch white pom-pom

6 × 12-inch piece lavender fun foam

18 inches moire ribbon, 1½ inches wide

Heavy thread (or dental floss)

Accessories: mini basket, eggs, flocked chick, flowers

1 Lightly sand wood edges and wipe with tack cloth to remove dust. Base paint both sides and edges of all pieces with gesso. Let dry.

2 Using patterns, cut out two ears and eyelid oval from white fun foam.

3 Rub a cotton ball on pastel chalk cube. Buff edges of rabbit with lavender chalk on cotton ball. Highlight front and back outside borders (reload color if necessary) until you have a softly colored edge. Buff center of foam ears in the same manner with pink chalk.

4 Assemble the bunny using high-temp setting for a stronger bond. Position and glue arms. Glue egg half to side of body (two inches in from bottom edge, one inch in from tail, with pointed end pointing to tail). Glue leg to prepared side by applying glue to egg and back edge at point of contact (to angle leg). Repeat on other leg.

5 Spray bunny with clear acrylic spray.

6 Cut off shaft from animal eyes and glue eyes to sides of face. Cut eyelid in half per pattern and glue to top halves of eyes. Glue pink nose pom in place. Fold narrow ends of ears in half and glue in ear holes. Glue on white tail pom.

7 For hat, cut 4-inch circle using pattern and 2½ × 7-inch band from lavender foam. Overlap and glue 2½-inch band edges. Apply glue to one end of band circle and glue to scrap of fun foam. Let cool, then trim. Star cut center of 4-inch brim circle; apply glue to open end of hat crown; center on brim. Let cool; increase center star slices to crown edges. Add ribbon band around crown and glue to head.

8 Cut out lavender foam collar using pattern. Spot glue collar to sides of neck. Overlap and glue four-inches of ribbon for tie, pinch in center, and wrap center tightly with heavy thread (or dental floss). Wrap a narrow strand of foam around thread and glue in place. Glue bow tie to neck.

9 Wrap handle of mini basket with ribbon. Tie handle to one hand of bunny. Glue Easter goodies into basket.

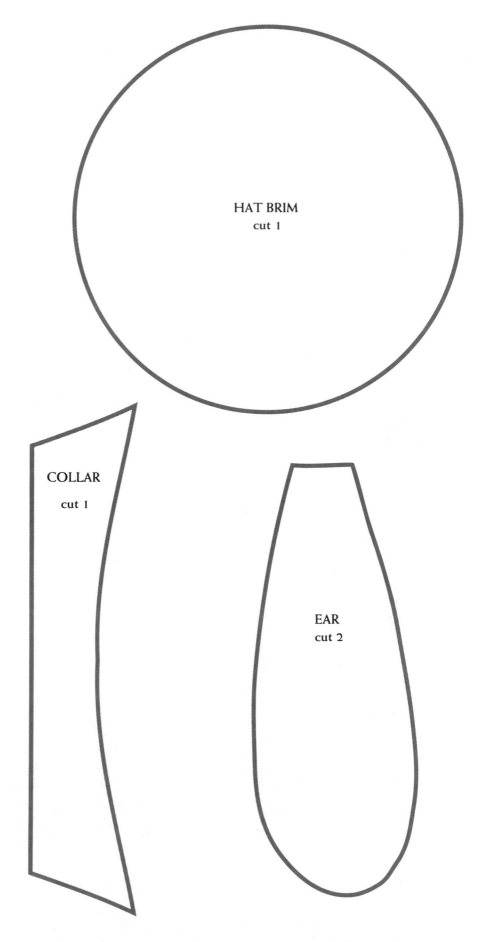

HAT BRIM
cut 1

COLLAR

cut 1

EAR
cut 2

EYELID

cut 1   cut line

Bunny Swag

These cheerful bunnies not only look great at
Easter—wouldn't they make a great baby
shower gift any time of the year?

What You'll Need

16-inch square each of green, peach, blue, pink, and yellow small print fabric

Marking pen or pencil

Sewing machine

Scissors

Fiberfill

White thread and needle

2 plastic rings

2/3 yard white gathered lace, 3/4 inch wide

15 inches each of green (double amount), peach, blue, and pink satin ribbon, 1/4 inch wide

1 Prewash and iron all fabric. Draw template from pattern; cut out. Double each fabric piece, with right sides together. Trace outline of template to wrong side of fabric piece. Sew on line. Cut outside of line with scant 1/4-inch seam allowance. Clip angles and curves. Turn right side out.

2 Stuff each bunny flat but firm with fiberfill. Slipstitch opening closed.

3 Sew bunnies together nose to tail. Sew rings to back of first and last bunny.

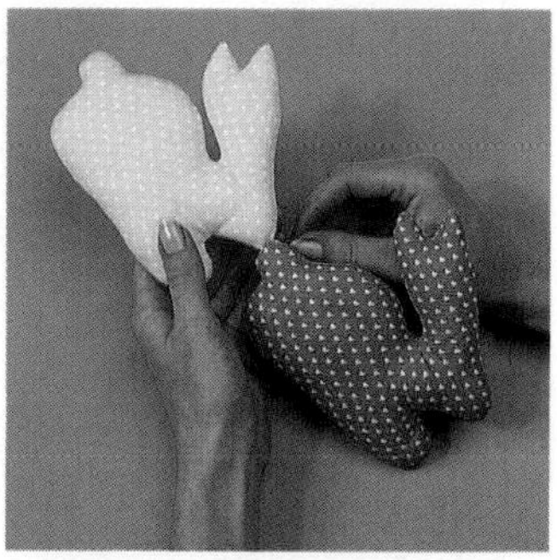

4 Cut five 4-inch lengths of gathered lace. Sew front of lace to back of ribbon, allowing for ties. Tie ribbon around neck of each bunny.

Placemat Set

Set a festive table with this colorful placemat

and napkin, accented with pretty lambs.

Your child will love eating off this!

What You'll Need

1 yard purple material

½ yard yellow material

¼ yard pink material

14 × 19-inch piece needle-punched batting

1 yard two-sided, paper-backed adhesive

½ yard adhesive-backed fleece

½ yard heavyweight stablizer

⅛ yard water-soluble embroi'ery facing

Purple, pink, and green thread to match material

½ yard purple satin ribbon, ⅛ inch wide

1 package jumbo emerald green rickrack

Sewing machine

Rotary cutter and cutting pad

Marking pen or pencil

Scissors

Toilet paper core

Tacky glue

1 Cut the placemat pieces from fabric. From the purple material, cut one 18¼ × 12½-inch rectangle and four 15 × 2½-inch strips. From the yellow material, cut a 14½ × 8½-inch rectangle. Cut a 5-inch square from the pink fabric.

2 All seam allowances are ¼ inch. Sew on top and bottom border to the 14½-inch sides of the yellow fabric (be sure to sew with right sides together and center strips). Sew side borders on each side. Place sewn piece over batting. Lightly glue edges in place. With right sides together, place 18¼ × 12½-inch purple rectangle on top and sew. Leave enough space unsewn so you can turn. Trim corners and batting. Turn inside out and slip stitch closing shut. Iron.

3 Draw lamb template from pattern on next page and cut out. Fuse adhesive-backed fleece to five-inch square of pink fabric. Fuse paper-backed adhesive to fleece. Trace pattern to paper side. Cut out.

4 Position lamb on placemat. Remove paper backing. Before fusing, place one end of rickrack underneath lamb's rump at border. Pin rickrack around border, to make sure corners form points. Fuse lamb in place according to manufacturer's instructions.

5 Place embroidery facing on top of lamb. Satin stitch around lamb with matching thread. Tear away facing.

6 Sew on rickrack along border with matching thread. Make a simple bow from purple ribbon. Sew to lamb.

7 For the napkin, cut four 2½ × 19-inch strips of purple fabric and one 18-inch square of yellow fabric. Press under one long edge of border.

57

8 Pin borders to each edge of yellow fabric, with raw edges matching. Sew borders around square. Turn to right side and iron. Iron seams toward purple fabric. Sew purple border on top of yellow fabric, keeping as close to purple edge as possible.

9 For napkin ring, cut 1½ inches off a toilet paper core. Cover core with a strip of batting, using tacky glue. Cut a 4 × 6-inch square of fabric and glue fabric to core using tacky glue.

10 For napkin ring lamb: Apply adhesive-backed fleece to one five-inch square of pink fabric (wrong side). To other five-inch square, apply fusible webbing to wrong side. Fuse webbing to heavyweight stabilizer. Apply fusible webbing to wrong side of stablized fabric. With wrong sides together, fuse fleece to webbing. Pink fabric should be on either side with layers of webbing and fleece in the middle.

11 Use pattern for lamb and trace on fabric. Satin stitch around lamb. Carefully trim fabric outside of satin stitch. Make a simple bow out of purple ribbon. Glue ribbon to lamb's neck and glue lamb to fabric-covered circle.

Mini Scene on the Half Shell

Fluffy bunnies and chicks are nestled in a

decorated half shell. Why not slip one into

an Easter basket for someone special?

What You'll Need

Plastic half shell eggs (with stage platform)

Wood body shapes

Acrylic paint: yellow, white, black

Small flat paintbrush

Fabric scraps of mini print material

Pinking shears

Sewing needle and thread

2-temp glue gun, glue sticks

Tacky glue

White bunny pom-poms: ¾ inch, four 7mm, 3mm

White baby bunny pom-poms: two 7mm, nine 3mm, four 5mm

Yellow chick pom-poms: ¾ inch, two ¼ inch

2 white bumpy chenille stems

Pink pastel chalk

Cotton balls

Black glass beads

1-inch orange chenille stem

Scissors

Decorating accessories: 1-inch sinamay hat, ribbon, mini eggs

Fabric paint (assorted colors)

1 Paint wood body white for bunny or yellow for chick. Let dry. With pinking shears, cut material into 1 × 6-inch piece. Use long sewing stitch to gather material strip on six-inch edge, pull tight, and sew ends together, forming a circle.

2 Assemble animal bodies using glue gun (and tacky glue on small parts) by putting dress on the body and a ¾-inch pom-pom on top (pom-pom will cover gathers).

3 For the bunny, glue a 7mm pom-pom on each side of dress for arms. Then glue two 7mm poms side by side on front of head for muzzle. Glue nose pom (3mm) on top middle of muzzle. Cut two bump sections from chenille stems for each ear; fold into V and glue to center top of head. Dust ears and muzzle with pink chalk and cotton balls. Glue on glass beads for eyes with tacky glue.

4 For chick, shape two ¼-inch poms for wings (cut on both sides of pom—from center to one edge forming a pointed wedge). Glue wings to back. Fold chenille stem in half and then in half again, forming a beak. Glue beak to lower part of head. Glue beads for eyes above beak.

5 To assemble baby bunny, (using tacky glue) glue two 7mm poms together for head and body. Glue four 5mm poms to body for arms and legs. Glue two 3mm poms to head for muzzle. Glue one 3mm pom to muzzle for nose. Glue three 3mm poms on top of each other and then to top side of head for ear. Repeat for other ear. Glue beads to head for eyes. Glue baby to mother's arm.

6 Assemble scene on half shell. Glue animal to shell's stage. Make a simple three loop bow, tie with thread, and glue to back side of animal. Add mini eggs, flowers, carrots, or other decorations.

7 Print spring greeting (or name for placecard) or spring design (carrot, flowers, hearts) on side of egg with fabric paint. Let dry.

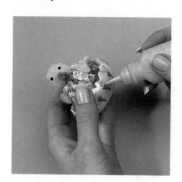

Easter Greetings

What better way to greet the ones you love than
with a handmade card. It will be treasured for
the care and concern you put into it!

What You'll Need

Note cards with trifold and
3 × 5-inch insert on
front panel

Ecru perforated paper

#24 tapestry needle

Embroidery floss: black;
dark green; gold; dark,
medium, light, very light of
coral and purple

Pencil with eraser

Scissors

Double-stick tape

1 Cut four pieces of
perforated paper 53 × 81
squares.

2 Find center of paper
horizontally and verti-
cally and mark lightly
with pencil. Find center
of chart by using arrows
to determine where to
begin stitching. Stitch
with two of six strands of
floss. Work cross-stitch-
ing first, then backstitching. Take care not to
carry floss across blank
areas behind design.

3 When stitching is
completed, insert paper
into note card, securing
in place with double-
stick tape.

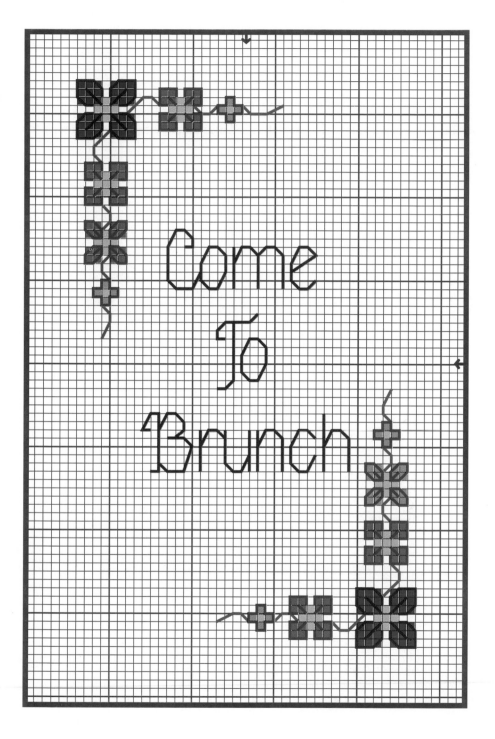

Dark coral
Medium coral
Light coral
Very light coral
Green
Yellow

Medium blue
Medium purple
Light purple
Very light purple
Black
Green
Yellow